Edwin Land

A Visionary's Quest for Instantaneous Innovation

By

Bram L. Alaric

Bram L. Alaric

Copyright

This book is copyrighted. No portion of this work may be copied, reproduced, or distributed in any form or by any means, including electronic, mechanical, or otherwise, without the prior written permission of the author. Exceptions are made for brief quotations in book reviews or similar uses, as permitted by law.

Disclaimer

This book is a reflection of the author's personal experiences and perspectives. Any similarities to persons, living or deceased, or real-life events are entirely coincidental. The author and publisher assume no responsibility for any errors or omissions, or for any outcomes resulting from the use of this information.

All rights reserved. © Bram L. Alaric, 2024.

Table of Contents

Introduction 3
A Bright Beginning 10
The Harvard Years 16
First Light: The Birth of Polaroid 23
Seeing beyond the surface 30
The Snap Revolution 37
Instant Innovation 44
The genius behind the curtain 52
Expanding Polaroid's Horizons 59
War & Peace 65
The Creative Mind 71
Facing Competition 78
Trials of Technology 84
A Lifetime of Influence 91
Beyond Polaroids 97
The Legacy of A Visionary 104
Conclusion 111

Introduction

Edwin Land is a towering figure in the pantheon of transformative inventors, a man whose vision changed the way humanity captures and experiences historical moments. Few people have so thoroughly intertwined science, art, and practicality into works that transcend generations. To many, he is simply the father of instant photography, but understanding Land's significance requires a glimpse into a mind that not only revolutionized an industry but also redefined the possibilities of human ingenuity itself.

On a chilly day in February 1947, at a scientific meeting in New York City, Land laid the groundwork for his groundbreaking achievements. A group of engineers, artists, and skeptics had gathered, drawn by rumors of a photographic miracle. They sat in silent anticipation as Land, an enigmatic figure with a flair for showmanship, walked to the podium. He demonstrated a device that promised to do the seemingly impossible: a camera capable of producing a fully developed photograph within sixty seconds of pressing the shutter.

As Land clicked the shutter on this revolutionary prototype, the entire room held its breath. A few moments later, he peeled back the paper frame to reveal an image: black-and-white, grainy by modern standards, but undeniably instant. Applause reverberated throughout the room, replacing gasps of disbelief. In that moment, Land had not only unveiled a technological marvel but also given the world a new perspective on the relationship between creativity and immediacy.

The journey to that historic demonstration began decades ago, with a curious boy whose fascination with light and optics shaped his future. Land's early years were characterized by an insatiable curiosity about how light interacted with his surroundings. While other children marveled at the vibrant colors of rainbows, Land sought to unravel their mysteries. This unrelenting drive led him to Harvard, where his ideas about polarizing light—a concept previously restricted to scientific theory—began to emerge.

However, Land's path was anything but ordinary. He left Harvard without a degree, determined to pursue his ideas on his own terms. At a time when most young men sought the security of established careers, Land chose to be an independent inventor. He pursued his research obsessively, frequently disappearing into his laboratory for days at a time. This singular focus quickly paid off, as he created the world's first low-cost polarizing filter. The breakthrough paved the way for countless applications, ranging from sunglasses to camera lenses, and established the Polaroid Corporation.

Land's genius was not limited to scientific discovery; it also included his ability to envision how his innovations could benefit people's lives. The invention of instant photography was more than just a technological achievement; it was a response to a deep human desire. According to Land, the idea came to him while on vacation in Santa Fe, New Mexico, in 1943. His young daughter questioned why she couldn't see the photograph he had just taken of her. That innocent question triggered a moment of revelation. Why couldn't photography be done immediately? Why should anyone have to wait days—or even hours—for a captured memory to appear?

The question consumed him, and for the next four years, he and his team worked tirelessly to turn their ideas into reality. The invention of the instant camera involved a complex interplay of chemistry, engineering, and artistry. It required not only the development of new materials but also the ability to smoothly synchronize complex processes within a single device. Land's leadership during this time was nothing short of visionary. He inspired his team with a simple mantra: "Don't take on a project unless it's clearly important and nearly impossible."

By the time the first Polaroid camera was released in 1948, it was clear that Edwin Land had discovered something profound. Instant photography was not just a convenience; it was an experience. For the first time, people could see their memories come to life in front of their eyes. It became a phenomenon, embraced by amateur and professional photographers alike, as well as artists such as Andy Warhol, who saw the Polaroid camera as a medium for creative expression.

Land's ability to combine scientific rigor with a profound understanding of human emotion distinguished him from other inventors of his time. He didn't just make products; he created experiences that delighted and inspired. He believed in making science more accessible and engaging, and he gave his product launches a theatrical flair, making them feel more like performances than presentations. This unique combination of intellect and charisma earned him admiration not only from the general public but also from the greatest minds of his time, such as Albert Einstein and Ansel Adams.

However, Land was not content to rest on his laurels. The introduction of the instant camera was just one chapter in a decades-long career that included advances in fields ranging from military optics to color imaging. He was a relentless innovator who believed that technology should serve a higher purpose. "We must always consider," he once said, "not only what the photograph is of, but what it is about." This philosophy reflected his dedication to pushing boundaries and exploring the intersection of science and art.

Edwin Land's story is one of audacity, brilliance, and a firm belief that the impossible is often simply the untried. His contributions to technology and society are lasting, but what truly distinguishes him is the way he saw the world—not as it was, but as it might be. As you read this book, you will travel through the life of a man who altered how we see and capture the world, a visionary who pushed the boundaries of what is possible, inspiring generations to dream bigger.

The image Land displayed on that February day in 1947 was more than just a photograph; it was a promise. A promise that innovation could bring the far away closer, the fleeting eternal, and the imagined real. Edwin Land fulfilled that promise, not only with his instant camera but also with a legacy of creativity and daring that continues to illuminate the path for both dreamers and doers today.

Chapter 1
A Bright Beginning

Edwin Herbert Land was born on May 7, 1909, in Bridgeport, Connecticut, to a family who encouraged his natural curiosity and desire to explore. His father, Harry Land, was a successful scrap metal merchant, while his mother, Martha Goldfaden, was a homemaker. Though their household lacked extraordinary material wealth, it was rich in values such as hard work and education. Edwin's parents instilled in him the value of discipline and perseverance, traits that would become hallmarks of his personality and accomplishments.

Even as a young boy, Edwin demonstrated the exceptional mind that would later redefine industries. His interest in light and optics began early, fueled by his desire to tinker with objects in his surroundings. Friends and family frequently commented on his ability to disassemble and reassemble devices with an intuitive understanding far beyond his years. Unlike other children who might become bored or frustrated, Edwin enjoyed investigating the mechanics of flashlights, prisms, and mirrors, frequently experimenting to learn how light behaved.

Land's formative years in Bridgeport occurred during the early twentieth century, when electricity, automobiles, and mass communication were transforming daily life. This period of rapid technological advancement undoubtedly had an impact on him, fostering an environment in which innovation was both celebrated and expected. For young Edwin, the world seemed full of limitless possibilities, and he approached it with an insatiable curiosity that drove him to think outside the box.

One watershed moment in Land's childhood occurred when he came across a physics book in his father's library. The book was dense with technical jargon, which most boys his age couldn't understand. But Edwin was unlike most boys. He studied its contents with unwavering determination, his interest focused on a single concept: light polarization. This principle, which describes the orientation of light waves, struck a deep chord with him. While most children would have moved on to more accessible interests, Edwin became obsessed with how light could be manipulated and controlled—a curiosity that would shape his life's work.

Visits to New York City with his family fueled Land's fascination with light even more. He would be mesmerized by the city's dazzling displays of neon signs and electric billboards, marveling at how light could be used for more than just illumination, but also communication and artistry. These experiences, combined with his innate ability to solve problems, laid the groundwork for his lifelong interest in optics.

Despite his growing interest in science, Edwin's academic years were not always easy. While he excelled in physics and mathematics, he became frustrated with traditional education's rigid structures. Teachers struggled to channel his boundless energy and unconventional thinking, but those who saw his potential encouraged him to pursue his passions. His intense focus on complex problems, as well as his refusal to accept easy answers, began to distinguish him from his peers.

Edwin's early personality was also heavily influenced by his family life. His father's entrepreneurial spirit and problem-solving mindset influenced him greatly. Harry Land was a practical man who was quick to solve problems in his business. Edwin absorbed these traits, learning to see obstacles as opportunities for invention rather than barriers. Meanwhile, his mother provided a counterbalance by encouraging him to pursue creativity and the arts, which added a sense of balance to his scientific endeavors.

As Edwin grew older, his experiments became more ambitious. By his adolescence, he was creating his own optical devices in a makeshift laboratory at home. Friends say he would spend hours lost in thought, often sketching diagrams or jotting down ideas in notebooks. For Land, light was more than just a scientific phenomenon; it was a language, a medium through which he could comprehend and shape the world.

One particularly interesting anecdote from this time period concerns Edwin's first attempt to create a polarizing filter. Using household items and improvised tools, he attempted to align microscopic particles in a way that would polarize light. Though his initial attempts were unsuccessful, the experience taught him two invaluable lessons: the value of perseverance and the need to think creatively about resources. This ability to innovate within constraints would eventually become one of his greatest strengths.

Bridgeport, while nurturing in many ways, was unable to contain Edwin Land's growing intellect and ambition. By the time he graduated from high school, everyone who knew him knew he was destined for great things. His parents encouraged him to pursue higher education, believing that a formal academic setting would provide him with the necessary tools and mentorship to channel his talents. Edwin saw Harvard University as the next logical step, as it was at the time a beacon of scientific research and discovery.

Edwin packed his bags for Cambridge, Massachusetts, carrying not only his dreams as a young scientist, but also his upbringing's lessons: the value of hard work, the beauty of curiosity, and the power of imagination. Little did anyone realize that this young man from Bridgeport would soon embark on a journey that would redefine photography, revolutionize optics, and cement his place in history as one of the most innovative minds of the twentieth century.

In the following chapter, we will follow Edwin Land as he begins his transformative years at Harvard, where his unconventional thinking will clash with traditional academia, setting him on a path that will eventually lead to the establishment of the Polaroid Corporation. It's a story about risk, rebellion, and the unwavering pursuit of innovation.

Chapter 2
The Harvard Years

Edwin Land arrived at Harvard University in 1926 as a young man full of ambition and boundless curiosity about the natural world. For many, Harvard's ivy-covered walls and intellectual energy represented the pinnacle of academic achievement, a place where the brightest minds gathered to discover the mysteries of science and philosophy. For Land, however, it was both an opportunity and a challenge, one that would expose the limitations of traditional education and propel him into a life of self-discovery.

Harvard's physics department, known for its rigorous curriculum, gave Edwin access to some of the best minds and resources of the time. Surrounded by students who shared his intellectual curiosity, he embraced the academic environment with zeal. However, cracks in his relationship with traditional academia appeared quickly. While others appeared content to absorb lectures and conduct prescribed experiments, Land felt constrained by the structure of his classes. The rigid frameworks and established methods of scientific exploration clashed with his innate desire to ask new questions and explore uncharted territory.

However, one subject continued to captivate him: light polarization. Scientists have known about polarization, a phenomenon that describes the alignment of light waves, for centuries, but it remained an untapped area for research and practical application. For Land, it was more than a theoretical curiosity; it was a gateway to comprehending and manipulating the very essence of light. He became obsessed with the idea of developing a practical polarizing filter—something that could turn this obscure concept into a tool for everyday use.

Land's dissatisfaction with Harvard's educational philosophy grew as he learned more about it. He frequently found that the answers given in textbooks or by professors were inadequate. To him, they represented the past—a summary of what was already known, rather than a challenge to discover what could still be understood. Land's mind, always restless, demanded more. It desired freedom from the constraints of lecture halls and lab manuals. Harvard's prestigious classrooms, for all their opulence, began to feel like a prison to the young inventor.

Land's dissatisfaction peaked during his sophomore year. He decided that he could no longer limit himself to a traditional academic path and made the bold and unconventional decision to drop out of Harvard. Many people were shocked by this decision, which served as a declaration of independence. Land believed that true discovery required the courage to deviate from established systems, even those as prestigious as Harvard. For him, leaving university was not an abandonment of learning, but rather an embrace of a different type of education—one guided by curiosity and experimentation rather than textbooks and exams.

Land, free of academic constraints, moved to New York City and began conducting his own polarized light experiments. Working in an improvised laboratory, often with equipment he had built himself, he embarked on a journey to make his theoretical ideas a reality. During this time, Land made his first major breakthrough: he discovered a way to make a low-cost, practical polarizing filter out of microscopic crystals embedded in a transparent sheet.

The innovation was groundbreaking. Traditional polarizing filters were costly and inconvenient, limiting their use to specific applications. In contrast, Land's invention was simple, low-cost, and versatile. The potential applications included sunglasses, camera lenses, and even scientific instruments. Land's achievement established him as a true pioneer, capable of bridging the gap between theoretical science and practical application.

This breakthrough was not only a testament to Land's intellectual abilities but also a reflection of his distinct approach to problem solving. Unlike many inventors who worked alone, Land thrived on collaboration. He sought out mentors, colleagues, and friends who could challenge and improve his thinking. During his time in New York, he met a network of scientists and innovators who supported his efforts and provided valuable feedback.

By the time Land returned to Harvard in 1929 to finish his studies, he had changed from the student who had left three years before. He was now a young scientist with a clear idea of what he wanted to accomplish. Though he resumed his studies, it became clear that the university could not accommodate his full range of ambitions. His enthusiasm for discovery extended far beyond the classroom, and his mind was already racing with ideas about how his divisive technology could change the world.

Land's second stint at Harvard proved to be short. Within a year, he had left the university permanently, this time with a clearer sense of purpose. He was prepared to take the next step in his journey, armed with the knowledge he had gained through both formal education and independent experiments. Harvard provided him with tools and ideas, but it was outside its walls that he realized his full potential.

Edwin Land's departure from Harvard signaled the start of a new chapter in his life, one defined by his unwavering pursuit of innovation. His work with polarized light laid the groundwork for a career that would soon revolutionize not only science but also how people perceived the world around them. His belief in the power of independent thought, as well as his willingness to question conventions, became central to his identity as an inventor and leader.

As Land prepared to take his first steps into the professional world, his vision began to form. He envisioned a future in which technology could boost human creativity and solve practical problems. With this dream in mind, he co-founded Land-Wheelwright Laboratories in 1932, which would eventually become the Polaroid Corporation.

In the following chapter, we will look at the history of Polaroid and the events that led to its first major breakthrough. "First Light: The Birth of Polaroid" will walk readers through the company's early days, the challenges Land faced in making his ideas a reality, and the moment his vision began to shine for the world to see.

Chapter 3
First Light: The Birth of Polaroid

The year 1937 was a watershed moment in Edwin Land's life and career, as well as the world of scientific innovation. At the age of 28, Land co-founded the Polaroid Corporation, which started as a small laboratory and grew into a cultural and technological powerhouse. The company was founded on Land's earlier breakthroughs in polarizing light, which had already established him as a brilliant thinker and problem solver. However, the path to Polaroid's inception and early success was anything but straightforward. It was a story of never-ending experimentation, unwavering determination, and the courage to pursue a vision that others struggled to understand.

Years of research culminated in Land's discovery of a practical polarizing material. In his makeshift lab in New

York City, he had successfully embedded microscopic herapathite crystals in transparent plastic sheets. This breakthrough enabled him to design a polarizing filter that was inexpensive, lightweight, and scalable, making it suitable for a variety of commercial and scientific applications. For the first time, the theoretical principles of light polarization could be applied in practical, everyday tools.

This innovation opened up new possibilities, but Land quickly realized that scientific discovery alone would not suffice. To share his invention with the world, he required a platform that combined scientific rigor with business acumen. In 1932, he formed a partnership with George Wheelwright III, a former Harvard roommate and entrepreneur. Their complementary skills—Land's technical prowess and Wheelwright's financial and operational knowledge—formed the foundation of what would become Polaroid. They initially established the Land-Wheelwright Laboratories to refine and commercialize the polarizing technology.

Their venture faced numerous challenges during its early years. While polarizing materials had numerous applications, convincing industries and consumers of their value proved difficult. Outside of academia, the concept of polarized light was poorly understood, so Land had to bridge the gap between scientific innovation and real-world practicality. His first major task was to determine which markets could benefit from his invention.

Polarized sunglasses were one of the initial items launched by Polaroid. Land recognized an immediate need for eyewear that could reduce glare from reflective surfaces, a problem that plagued drivers and pilots throughout the increasingly motorized 1930s. He worked tirelessly to perfect the product, demonstrating its effectiveness at trade shows, industry gatherings, and even on Boston's streets, where he would stop passersby to demonstrate the impact of polarization.

Despite the product's utility, the public's understanding of the technology was limited, and initial sales were modest. To make matters worse, the Great Depression reduced consumer spending, making any new and unfamiliar product a difficult sell. However, Land remained undeterred. He believed in the transformative power of his technology and remained dedicated to his vision.

As Polaroid's portfolio grew, so did Land's reputation as a scientific innovator. His polarizing filters were used in a variety of applications beyond sunglasses, including photographic equipment, scientific instruments, and military devices. During this time, Land's communication skills began to shine. He had a unique ability to explain complex concepts in a way that was both accessible and inspiring. Whether speaking to potential investors, government officials, or fellow scientists, Land's enthusiasm for his work was contagious, and it helped secure critical support for Polaroid's early efforts.

One of the company's most significant breakthroughs occurred when it formed a partnership with the United States military. The rising tensions of the pre-World War II era created a demand for advanced optical devices, and Polaroid's polarizing filters were invaluable in applications such as aerial reconnaissance and submarine periscopes. These contracts were a critical financial lifeline for the fledgling company, helping to establish Polaroid as a serious player in the technology industry.

The military partnership also signaled the start of Land's larger role in national security and defense innovation, a theme that would continue throughout his career. It was here that he demonstrated his ability to not only create groundbreaking technologies but also predict their strategic significance. His work with the military solidified his reputation as a scientist capable of applying theoretical principles to urgent real-world problems.

Despite these early successes, Land remained intent on pushing the limits of what his polarizing materials could accomplish. He saw Polaroid as more than a business; it was a platform for innovation, a place where ideas could grow and take shape. Land fostered a collaborative and experimental environment by hiring talented researchers and encouraging them to take on bold, ambitious projects. It was a culture that valued creativity alongside technical expertise, and it laid the groundwork for the revolutionary inventions that would soon emerge from Polaroid's labs.

By the late 1930s, Polaroid had evolved from a small laboratory to a thriving company with a growing portfolio of products and applications. Land's vision of making science practical and accessible was gaining traction, and his unwavering determination inspired those around him. He had demonstrated how polarizing technology could transform industries, but he was far from done.

The initial period of Polaroid showcased Land's conviction in the importance of innovation and the significance of determination. He had successfully turned a niche scientific concept into a thriving business, overcoming financial difficulties, consumer skepticism, and technical challenges along the way. Throughout it all, Land's unwavering belief in his ideas and ability to adapt to new situations established him as one of the most promising inventors of his generation.

As Polaroid entered the 1940s, Land's ambitions expanded even more. His work with polarized materials was just the beginning. He imagined a future in which technology could not only solve practical problems but also boost human creativity and expression. This vision would inspire him to invent instant photography, which would define his career and change the world.

In the following chapter, "Seeing Beyond the Surface," we will look at how Land's restless curiosity and pioneering spirit led to the development of new optical technologies, as well as his pivotal role in advancing military and commercial innovation during World War II. This period would not only put his ingenuity to the test but also reveal the breadth of his vision for what Polaroid—and science itself—could accomplish.

Chapter 4
Seeing beyond the surface

As the world descended into chaos during World War II, Edwin Land found himself at the crossroads of innovation and necessity. The war demanded unprecedented technological advances, and Land's optics expertise quickly drew the attention of military leaders. What began as a company focused on polarized lenses and commercial applications quickly grew into an important partner for the United States military. During this transformative period, Land's ingenuity and unwavering pursuit of perfection not only increased Polaroid's significance but also helped reshape the role of science in war.

Polaroid's collaboration with the military began with a problem that was both practical and urgent: increasing visibility for soldiers and pilots. Land's polarizing filters, originally designed for sunglasses and cameras, proved to be life-saving on the battlefield. These filters reduced glare, allowing pilots to see more clearly under bright and reflective conditions, which was a significant advantage in aerial combat and navigation. Polaroid technology quickly became indispensable, and Land's reputation as a scientific innovator grew as his work saved lives.

Land's most significant wartime contribution was the creation of polarizing filters for aircraft instruments. During flight, pilots frequently encountered harsh glare from sunlight reflecting off clouds or water, which could obscure critical information on their instrument panels. By adding polarizing filters to these displays, Land enabled pilots to read their instruments with precision, even in difficult conditions. This innovation not only improved flight safety, but it also increased military operational effectiveness.

The applications of Polaroid technology went far beyond the skies. Submarines, which were becoming an increasingly important component of naval warfare, benefited from Land's experience. Traditional submarine periscopes suffered from glare, making it difficult for operators to identify enemy ships and navigate safely. Land's polarizing materials transformed these periscopes, dramatically improving visibility and giving them a significant advantage in underwater operations. The United States integrated Polaroid filters into submarine optics. The Navy gained a technological advantage, which proved invaluable in the Atlantic and Pacific theaters.

Land's contributions during the war were not limited to existing technologies; he also oversaw completely new projects. One notable achievement was the creation of stereoscopic rangefinders, which used polarized light to measure distances with remarkable precision. This technology was used in artillery targeting and other military applications, highlighting the versatility and significance of Polaroid's innovations.

Throughout the war, Land worked tirelessly, frequently pushing himself and his teammates to their limits. He firmly believed that scientists had a responsibility to contribute to the greater good, and he approached his work with urgency and purpose. He understood the importance of wartime innovation: each advancement could mean the difference between victory and defeat, life and death.

Land's leadership during this period demonstrated not only his technical prowess but also his ability to inspire those around him. Polaroid's labs became hubs of creativity and collaboration, with scientists, engineers, and technicians working together to address some of the war's most pressing challenges. Land's approach to problem-solving was both unconventional and effective; he encouraged his team to question assumptions, experiment with unconventional ideas, and embrace the unknown.

This wartime environment also allowed Land to fine-tune his philosophy of innovation. He believed that the most meaningful discoveries frequently came from the intersection of science and necessity. His work during World War II exemplified this principle, as he tailored his inventions to meet the military's immediate needs while also laying the groundwork for future advancements.

By the conclusion of the war, Polaroid had positioned itself as a significant contributor in the defense sector. The company's contributions to military optics have not only saved lives but also cemented its position as a technological innovator. Land emerged from the war as a national hero, known for his ability to bridge the gap between theoretical science and practical application.

Despite his wartime successes, Land was not one to dwell on the past. For him, the end of the war signaled the start of a new chapter, one full of untapped potential. While he was proud of Polaroid's contributions to the military, he wanted to shift the company's focus to peacetime applications. He imagined a future in which technology could serve not only the needs of governments but also the dreams and desires of ordinary citizens.

The seeds of this vision were planted long before the war, but they became clearer in the aftermath. Land's work with polarized light demonstrated the power of optics to change how people perceive the world, and he believed that this power could be used to create new forms of expression and connection. It was a bold and ambitious concept that would necessitate not only scientific innovation but also an understanding of human creativity.

As Polaroid evolved from a wartime innovator to a peacetime pioneer, Land laid the groundwork for his most famous invention: the instant camera. The concept of capturing and developing a photograph in real time was both revolutionary and ambitious, and it would quickly become Land's signature achievement. This invention would not only change the way people documented their lives, but it would also solidify Polaroid's legacy as a company that pushed the boundaries of possibility.

In the following chapter, "A Snap Revolution," we will look at the origins of instant photography and the incredible journey that led to the release of the first Polaroid camera. This period in Land's life represents a convergence of science, art, and imagination, as he sought to make the impossible possible and spread the magic of photography to millions of people around the globe.

Chapter 5
The Snap Revolution

One of Edwin Land's most transformative ideas emerged during a quiet family vacation in Santa Fe, New Mexico, in 1943. On a sunny afternoon, Land was photographing his young daughter, Jennifer. After he took a photograph, she innocently inquired as to why she couldn't see it right away. It was a simple, almost childlike question, but it resulted in a profound revelation for Land. Why can't photography be instantaneous? Why should people have to wait hours—or even days—for a tangible reminder of their experience?

That question planted a seed in Land's mind, which would sprout into a revolutionary idea. He began to envision a camera capable of developing its own film within moments of capturing an image, eliminating the need for a darkroom or third-party processing. It was an audacious concept that necessitated the seamless integration of chemistry, mechanics, and optics. Nonetheless, Land, who thrived on taking on the impossible, saw it as a worthwhile challenge.

Returning from his vacation, Land threw himself into the problem with his usual zeal. He assembled a team of scientists and engineers at Polaroid and set out to make his vision a reality. The workload was daunting. It necessitated developing a film that could carry both the negative and the developing chemicals, as well as designing a camera capable of carrying out multiple processes with precise timing. Land frequently collaborated with his team, sharing their frustrations and breakthroughs and encouraging them to think beyond conventional boundaries.

By 1947, after years of tireless experimentation and countless prototypes, the first Polaroid Land Camera was ready to be revealed. Land chose the Optical Society of America's annual meeting in New York City as its debut. Standing in front of an audience of scientists and industry leaders, he demonstrated the device with flair. After taking a photograph of the audience, he removed a print from the camera and, in just 60 seconds, peeled away the paper backing to reveal the developed image.

The audience was stunned. For a brief moment, there was silence, as if they couldn't believe what they had just witnessed. Then there was an eruption of applause, a wave of excitement that echoed far beyond the room. Land's invention was more than just a technological marvel; it was a foreshadowing of the future, a moment when science crossed over into magic.

In 1948, Polaroid introduced its first commercial instant camera, the Model 95, along with a special film designed for it. The camera, priced at $89.95—a considerable amount for that period—became an instant hit. Retailers were astounded when the initial supply sold out in minutes and customers demanded more. For many people, the Polaroid Land Camera was more than just a device; it was a portal to new forms of expression and creativity.

The mechanics of the instant camera were both elegant and complex. When the shutter was pressed, the film's negative captured the image. As the film was ejected from the camera, it passed through rollers that evenly distributed a layer of developing chemicals across its surface. In less than a minute, the picture showed up, seemingly out of nowhere. This process combined complex chemical reactions with precise engineering, demonstrating Land's ability to blend science and art into a cohesive whole.

Instant photography captured the public's imagination like no other innovation at the time. Users were impressed not only by the speed but also by the immediacy of the experience. People could now hold a memory in their hands moments after it happened, and share it with friends and family in real time. This sense of immediacy gave photography a more personal and spontaneous quality, transforming it from a formal process to an everyday activity.

Artists and professionals were equally captivated. Renowned photographers such as Ansel Adams used the Polaroid camera as a creative tool, praising its ability to capture fine details and tones. For Adams, instant photography was more than just a convenience; it was a tool for artistic exploration. Similarly, Andy Warhol incorporated Polaroid images into his iconic pop art, blurring the distinction between art and technology.

The influence of Polaroid on culture extended well beyond the realm of art. It became a staple at family gatherings, vacations, and celebrations, capturing memories that would otherwise be lost. The ability of the instant camera to produce tangible, physical prints struck a deep chord in an era before digital photography. Its influence spanned generations, allowing millions who had never considered themselves photographers to take up the art form.

Land's achievement was not only the invention of a new type of camera but also the redefining of what photography could be. He had simplified, accelerated, and magically transformed a process that had previously required expertise, time, and resources. The Polaroid camera was more than just a technological innovation; it was a cultural phenomenon that altered how people perceived and shared their surroundings.

However, for Land, the release of the instant camera was only the beginning. His mind was already racing with new ideas, new ways to improve the technology and broaden its applications. He imagined a future in which instant photography could be used in medicine, education, and industry, as a tool for solving real-world problems rather than simply capturing memories.

The success of the Polaroid Land Camera cemented Land's reputation as a visionary, capable of turning abstract ideas into transformative realities. However, it also increased the stakes for Polaroid. With the instant camera capturing the world's attention, the company was on track for unprecedented growth, but it also faced increased competition and expectations. Land recognized that staying ahead required constant innovation and a willingness to push the limits of what was possible.

In the following chapter, "Instant Innovation," we will look at the next stage of Land's journey, as he expanded Polaroid's vision and refined instant camera technology. From color photography breakthroughs to production scaling challenges, Land's unwavering drive to innovate would shape his company and redefine the art and science of photography.

Chapter 6
Instant Innovation

The year 1948 marked a watershed moment for Edwin Land and the Polaroid Corporation. After years of meticulous research, sleepless nights, and relentless experimentation, the world was introduced to the first commercial instant camera—the Polaroid Model 95. It was an invention that would not only revolutionize the photography industry but also change the way people lived and shared their experiences. For Land, the camera's launch marked the culmination of a bold vision and the start of a new era of innovation.

The Model 95 was first introduced during the holiday season at Jordan Marsh, a department store located in Boston. With its sturdy design, innovative mechanics, and revolutionary film, the instant camera promised to deliver what had previously appeared impossible: a developed photograph in 60 seconds. Land himself was present at the launch, giving live demonstrations to curious shoppers. The spectacle was captivating. Crowds gathered to watch Land take a photograph, remove the print, and peel back the paper to reveal the fully developed image. The atmosphere of amazement in the room was unmistakable.

The public's response was immediate and overwhelming. The first batch of 57 cameras sold out in a single day, demonstrating Land's invention's ability to capture consumers' imaginations. For many, the Polaroid camera was more than a product; it was an experience. It enabled people to hold their memories in their hands almost instantly, transforming photography from a time-consuming and distant process to something more immediate and personal.

Land's instant camera appealed to a wide range of users, from amateur photographers to experienced professionals. Families welcomed it as a means to preserve significant events and daily experiences. Photographers saw it as a creative tool that encouraged experimentation and spontaneity. Professionals in fields such as real estate, law enforcement, and medicine embraced the technology for its convenience and speed. Land redefined the purpose of photography by closing the gap between the act of taking a photograph and the act of viewing it.

However, the journey to achieving this success was far from easy. The Model 95's polished exterior conceals years of painstaking trial and error. Creating a film capable of capturing, processing, and developing an image in seconds was a tremendous technical challenge. It required the development of not only new photographic materials but also new chemical processes that could function seamlessly within a small system. Land and his team faced numerous setbacks while working to perfect the technology, frequently rejecting ideas that appeared promising on paper but failed in practice.

One of the most significant challenges was ensuring the consistency and dependability of the development process. Unlike traditional film, which was dependent on external darkroom conditions, instant film had to function flawlessly within the camera. The temperature, humidity, and light exposure required careful regulation. Each layer of the film—negative, developer, and positive—had to work together perfectly to produce a sharp, well-balanced image. Achieving this level of precision necessitated constant experimentation and innovation.

Land's leadership during this time was just as important as his technical knowledge. He fostered a culture of creativity and perseverance at Polaroid, encouraging his team to approach problems from various perspectives and to accept failure as part of the process. He frequently collaborated with his researchers, providing insights and solutions that helped the project move forward. His ability to inspire and challenge his team played a critical role in overcoming the technical challenges that threatened to derail the invention.

Another barrier was the cost of production. The instant camera and its accompanying film were difficult to manufacture, so Polaroid had to find ways to scale production without compromising quality. Land collaborated closely with engineers and designers to streamline the manufacturing process, ensuring that the technology was produced efficiently while remaining affordable to consumers. It was a delicate balance, but one that Polaroid achieved thanks to Land's foresight and determination.

The introduction of the Polaroid Model 95 necessitated a bold marketing strategy. Land recognized that his invention required more than just technical merit to succeed; it needed to connect with people on an emotional level. Polaroid's advertising campaigns emphasized the fun and spontaneity of instant photography, presenting the camera as a tool for capturing life's fleeting moments. The messaging resonated with the public, instilling a sense of wonder and excitement that fueled the brand's rapid expansion.

The instant camera's cultural impact grew alongside its popularity. Polaroid became synonymous with innovation and creativity, representing the fusion of science and art. Its technology enabled people to document their lives in real-time, resulting in a new style of storytelling that was both immediate and intimate. The instant photograph evolved beyond a product to become a cultural artifact, a tangible memory that could be shared and treasured.

The success of the Polaroid Model 95 signaled the start of a golden era for the company. Over the next few years, Polaroid introduced new models and expanded its product line, constantly refining technology to meet the demands of its expanding customer base. The introduction of color instant film in the 1960s was another watershed moment, cementing Polaroid's position as a pioneer in photographic innovation.

Edwin Land saw the launch of the first instant camera as a stepping stone rather than an endpoint. He saw the technology as a tool for further exploration, a way to push the limits of what photography could accomplish. His mind was already racing with ideas for new applications, ranging from scientific research to creative expression. The success of the Model 95 only fueled his ambition, inspiring him to dream bigger.

Nonetheless, the challenges of sustaining innovation were ever-present. Land understood that staying ahead required constant reinvention and the willingness to take risks. He remained deeply involved in the development process, constantly pushing his team to improve and broaden Polaroid's capabilities. His insatiable desire for perfection was both a strength and a liability, propelling the company to new heights while requiring extraordinary effort from everyone involved.

The story of instant photography demonstrates Land's ability to combine scientific brilliance with a deep understanding of human emotion. He invented not only a new type of camera but also a new way of seeing the world. By making photography more immediate and accessible, he elevated it from a technical process to a shared experience that brought people closer to their memories and one another.

In the following chapter, "The Genius Behind the Curtain," we will delve into Edwin Land's mind—his philosophy of innovation, his distinct leadership style, and the qualities that propelled him to the ranks of the twentieth century's most influential inventors. Behind Polaroid's public success was a man motivated by insatiable curiosity and a belief in the power of imagination to change the world.

Chapter 7
The genius behind the curtain

Edwin Land was more than just an inventor; he was a visionary leader who encouraged innovation and creativity at all levels of his organization. While the general public marveled at the wonders that Polaroid created, the true magic often occurred behind the scenes, where Land orchestrated a symphony of ideas, talent, and technology. His leadership style was distinctive, combining scientific rigor with theatrical flair, and it was critical to Polaroid's success as one of the most innovative companies of the twentieth century.

One of the most distinguishing features of Land's leadership was his ability to transform science into a performance. Land, known for his "scientific theater" presentations, captivated audiences by demonstrating complex technological breakthroughs in dramatic yet educational ways. These events were more than just product launches; they were moments of epiphany. Land would carefully stage his demonstrations to create suspense, walking his audience through the problem his team had solved before revealing the solution in a moment of surprise. Whether revealing the first instant photograph or a new advancement in optics, Land's presentations left audiences in awe and eager for more.

These performances were more than just marketing stunts; they demonstrated Land's profound understanding of the emotional power of science. He believed that innovation was more than just solving technical problems; it was also about inspiring people to see the world in new ways. His ability to communicate complex ideas clearly and passionately made him a charismatic figure capable of bridging the technical and emotional divide. Land's presentations reinforced Polaroid's identity as a company that achieved the impossible, inspiring both his employees and the general public.

Behind the scenes at Polaroid, Land created an environment unlike any other. He was a firm believer in interdisciplinary collaboration, frequently assembling teams of scientists, engineers, and artists to work on large projects. Land's approach to innovation was holistic, and he recognized that breakthroughs frequently occurred at the intersection of disciplines. By encouraging diverse perspectives and open dialogue, he fostered a culture of creativity.

Land's ability to motivate his team was based on his own boundless curiosity and enthusiasm. He saw every challenge as an opportunity for discovery, frequently immersing himself in the details of a project with his employees. He was known to spend long hours in the lab, interacting directly with researchers and providing insights that were frequently pivotal. His presence was both motivating and demanding; those who worked with him described him as a leader who expected excellence while also encouraging them to reach their full potential.

Land's leadership was built around his belief in the importance of vision. He frequently spoke of the need to pursue projects that were "manifestly important and nearly impossible," a phrase that summed up his ambition and willingness to take risks. Land encouraged his team to think boldly and tackle problems that others considered unsolvable. This philosophy not only drove Polaroid's most groundbreaking innovations, but it also instilled a sense of purpose and excitement among its employees.

Land's genius was enhanced by the extraordinary talent with which he surrounded himself. Key members of his team played critical roles in making his ideas a reality. Howard Rogers, a brilliant chemist, was one such individual who contributed to the development of the instant film that became the foundation of Polaroid's success. Rogers' chemical process expertise supplemented Land's visionary thinking, ensuring that Polaroid's innovations were as strong technically as they were conceptually.

Stanley Calderwood, Polaroid's marketing guru, was also a key collaborator. Calderwood recognized the emotional appeal of Land's inventions and worked tirelessly to establish Polaroid as a brand associated with creativity and innovation. His ability to turn technological breakthroughs into compelling narratives helped Polaroid capture the public's attention and build a loyal customer base.

Land was also inspired by artists such as Ansel Adams, the legendary photographer. Adams, who became a close friend and collaborator, used Polaroid cameras to push the limits of photographic art. His feedback on the capabilities and limitations of Polaroid technology was invaluable in informing the development of new products. Land saw these collaborations with artists as more than just refining technology; they were about exploring the deeper relationship between science and art.

Land's leadership style was not without challenges. His unwavering pursuit of perfection and high expectations may be demanding, even exhausting, for those around him. However, for many, working with Land was a once-in-a-lifetime experience. He had an uncanny ability to bring out the best in people, inspiring them to achieve things they never thought possible. Under his leadership, Polaroid became a hub for extraordinary ideas, constantly pushing the boundaries of what was possible to imagine and achieve.

Land's culture at Polaroid extended beyond the laboratory. He believed in the value of community and the role of businesses in contributing to society. Polaroid's headquarters in Cambridge, Massachusetts, became a center of intellectual and cultural activity, drawing thinkers and creators from all over the world. Land's impact went far beyond his company, influencing the broader landscape of innovation and inspiring a new generation of scientists, entrepreneurs, and artists.

Land's leadership role at Polaroid evolved as the company grew. He remained heavily involved in the company's creative and technical aspects, but he also became a figurehead, representing the power of vision and determination. His ability to balance these roles—to be both the genius behind the curtain and the face of the company—was a testament to his distinct combination of intelligence and charisma.

The story of Edwin Land's leadership is one of inspiration, collaboration, and an unwavering pursuit of excellence. He was a man who believed that science had the power to change the world, and he worked tirelessly to demonstrate this. Under his leadership, Polaroid not only revolutionized photography but also demonstrated the transformative power of innovation.

In the following chapter, "Expanding Polaroid's Horizons," we will look at how Land and his team pushed the boundaries of their technology even further, venturing into new markets and applications. From advances in color photography to experiments in 3D imaging, this period was one of growth and exploration for Polaroid, cementing its position as a global innovator.

Chapter 8
Expanding Polaroid's Horizons

Because of the success of its instant cameras, Polaroid Corporation had already become synonymous with groundbreaking photographic innovations in the 1950s and 1960s. However, Edwin Land saw science and technology as capable of much more than simply capturing images. Land saw Polaroid as more than just a camera company; it was a platform for exploring the frontiers of optics, chemistry, and materials science. Under his visionary leadership, Polaroid began to broaden its horizons, diversifying its product lines, and addressing challenges in fields as diverse as advanced imaging, sunglasses, and scientific education.

One of Polaroid's most notable ventures outside of instant photography was the development of 3D imaging technology. Land had long been fascinated by the relationship between light and perception, and he believed that 3D imaging could transform fields like medicine, engineering, and entertainment. Polaroid's efforts in this area resulted in the development of polarized lenses and projection systems, allowing audiences to see three-dimensional images with remarkable clarity. While 3D movies and displays were considered novelties at the time, Polaroid's contributions paved the way for future advances in immersive visual technologies.

At the same time, Polaroid continued to improve and expand its line of polarized sunglasses, which was one of the company's first and most enduring successes. Land's original invention of low-cost polarizing filters had already transformed the eyewear industry by significantly lowering glare and improving visual comfort. In the decades since, Polaroid sunglasses have become a must-have for drivers, pilots, and outdoor enthusiasts, combining functionality with sleek, modern design. Land's commitment to making high-quality optical technology available to the general public ensured that Polaroid sunglasses remained popular and affordable.

Polaroid also excelled at developing advanced films. While instant photography was the company's trademark, Land saw the potential for specialized films that could serve a variety of purposes. Polaroid introduced films for scientific research, medical imaging, and industrial applications, each tailored to the specific needs of professionals in those fields. These innovations not only broadened Polaroid's product line but also demonstrated the adaptability of its core technologies.

Polaroid's ability to diversify reflected Land's insatiable curiosity and refusal to be constrained by traditional business models. Unlike many executives who were solely concerned with profitability, Land was motivated by a desire to solve problems and test new ideas, no matter how unconventional they appeared. He believed that science should benefit humanity, and he frequently emphasized the importance of making complex technologies understandable and accessible to the general public.

Polaroid's commitment to education exemplified Land's vision of democratizing science. He saw Polaroid's products as more than just tools; they were also opportunities to inspire curiosity and creativity. Teachers and students, for example, embraced Polaroid instant cameras as a means of bringing abstract concepts to life. The photographs' immediacy enabled students to experiment and see the results of their work in real-time, fostering a better understanding of scientific principles.

Land believed that education was more than just disseminating information; it was also about empowering people to think critically and explore their surroundings. He frequently discussed the need to bridge the gap between science and the humanities, emphasizing the importance of creativity in driving innovation. Polaroid became a reflection of this philosophy, a company that combined art, science, and business to create functional and inspiring products.

The diversification of Polaroid's product lines demonstrated the company's ability to respond to changing markets and consumer demands. While instant photography remained its flagship product, Polaroid's expansion into eyewear, imaging systems, and specialized films kept it relevant in a rapidly changing technological landscape. Land's willingness to take risks and venture into uncharted territory kept Polaroid at the forefront of innovation even as competition increased.

Despite its successes, Polaroid faced a number of challenges during this time. Scaling production, managing costs, and ensuring product quality required constant vigilance. While Land's perfectionism drove Polaroid's success, it also put a lot of pressure on the company's employees and resources. Despite this, Polaroid thrived, fueled by Land's unwavering belief in the transformative power of science and technology.

Polaroid's expansion into new markets and technologies was more than just a business strategy; it reflected Edwin Land's overall vision for the future. He envisioned a world in which science was not limited to laboratories but was integrated into everyday life, and where innovation was not just the domain of experts but a shared endeavor that benefited all of humanity. This vision shaped every aspect of Polaroid's operations, from its ground-breaking products to its dedication to education and community engagement.

As the 1960s came to an end, Polaroid was at the pinnacle of its power, a company that had not only revolutionized photography but also redefined what it meant to be an innovator. Land's ability to push boundaries and inspire others had transformed Polaroid into a global leader, a company that exemplified the power of creativity and collaboration.

In the following chapter, "War and Peace," we will look at how Land's contributions went beyond commerce to issues of national importance. Land's impact on society extended far beyond the products he created, including his work with the United States military and his efforts to balance the demands of business and ethics. It was a period that put his ideals to the test and cemented his legacy as one of history's most influential thinkers.

Bram L. Alaric

Chapter 9
War & Peace

Edwin Land's genius was not limited to Polaroid's commercial innovations; it also had a significant impact on military technology during one of the most turbulent periods of the twentieth century. The Cold War was a period of high geopolitical tension, with the United States and the Soviet Union competing for technological and military superiority. In this environment, Land emerged as a trusted advisor and collaborator with the United States government, using his knowledge to create tools that would give the country a strategic advantage.

Land's involvement in national defense began during WWII, but it was during the Cold War that his contributions reached new heights. As a natural problem solver, he was drawn to the challenge of addressing the country's security needs through science and innovation. One of his most significant contributions was his research into aerial surveillance technology, which became a cornerstone of intelligence gathering during this period.

Land's efforts were centered on the U-2 spy plane, which combined his technological brilliance with a strong sense of patriotism. The U-2, designed by Lockheed's Skunk Works team and overseen by legendary engineer Kelly Johnson, was an aircraft capable of flying at altitudes greater than 70,000 feet—far beyond the reach of Soviet air defenses at the time. Land played a critical role in the project, contributing significantly to the development of the plane's sophisticated photographic and reconnaissance systems.

The U-2's camera technology was revolutionary, allowing the US to capture high-resolution images of Soviet installations and missile sites from previously unattainable heights. Land and his team collaborated closely with the military and intelligence agencies to perfect the camera's design, ensuring that it could function properly in extreme conditions. Land's contributions extended beyond technical details; he also advised government officials on the strategic importance of aerial surveillance and the need for rapid program development.

The success of the U-2 program marked a watershed moment in the Cold War. The intelligence it provided helped the US gain a better understanding of the Soviet Union's capabilities and intentions, allowing it to avoid potential conflicts and shape foreign policy decisions. For Land, the project demonstrated the power of science to address complex global issues. He believed strongly in scientists' responsibility to contribute to national security, and he approached his work on the U-2 with the same enthusiasm and dedication that he brought to Polaroid's innovations.

However, Land's involvement in defense projects was not without ethical quandaries. Balancing Polaroid's commercial interests with his research into military technology required careful consideration. While he was proud of the contributions his innovations had made to national security, he was also well aware of the potential consequences of his work. The surveillance technologies he helped develop were effective, but they also raised concerns about privacy, ethics, and the broader implications of technological progress.

Land wrestled with these issues throughout his career, attempting to strike a balance between his sense of duty and his dedication to the principles of transparency and creativity. He believed that science should ultimately benefit humanity, and he was deeply concerned about the possibility of technology being misused. These concerns influenced his approach to work, prompting him to advocate for ethical considerations in the development and implementation of new technologies.

Despite these obstacles, Land's contributions to national defense cemented his reputation as one of the most influential scientific minds of his time. His ability to bridge the gap between commercial innovation and military technology was unparalleled, and his contributions to the U-2 program were just one example of his influence. Land's influence extended to other defense initiatives, such as advanced optical systems and early reconnaissance satellites.

Throughout, Land remained deeply committed to Polaroid and its mission of innovation. He believed that the lessons he learned from his defense work could be applied to the company's commercial ventures, resulting in advances in photography and imaging technology. Much of his career was defined by the interplay of his roles as a scientist, inventor, and patriot, which demonstrated his ability to navigate the complexities of a rapidly changing world.

As the Cold War progressed, Land's contributions continued to shape Polaroid and the larger technological landscape. He worked tirelessly to ensure that his innovations served a larger purpose, whether in terms of national security or in the lives of ordinary people. His legacy as a pioneer in aerial surveillance technology is an important chapter in the history of science and defense, demonstrating the profound impact of his work on global security and politics.

In the following chapter, "The Creative Mind," we will look at the philosophies and principles that shaped Land's approach to innovation. From his belief in the power of interdisciplinary collaboration to his emphasis on creativity and exploration, this chapter will look at how Land's unique perspective influenced his work and inspired those around him. It is a story of insatiable curiosity, boundless imagination, and a strong desire to shape a better future through science and technology.

Chapter 10
The Creative Mind

Edwin Land had an insatiable curiosity, an unwavering ambition, and a unique understanding of the relationship between science and creativity. His approach to problem-solving, risk-taking, and innovation was more than a philosophy; it pervaded every aspect of his work at Polaroid and beyond. Land believed that creativity was the driving force behind all meaningful progress, and he dedicated his life to instilling it in himself, his teams, and the larger scientific community.

Land believed that creativity thrives at the intersection of curiosity and discipline. He frequently described innovation as a journey, beginning with a strong desire to understand how something worked or why a problem existed. Land saw curiosity as an active, driving force that compelled him to dig deeper, ask questions that others had overlooked, and investigate ideas that appeared impossible at first glance. This insatiable curiosity fueled some of his most revolutionary inventions, from polarized lenses to instant photography.

Land believed that the most significant breakthroughs came from tackling problems that were "manifestly important and nearly impossible." This philosophy guided his work at Polaroid, where he encouraged his teams to think boldly and take on challenges that others might have considered insurmountable. He recognized that achieving such lofty goals required not only technical expertise but also a willingness to embrace uncertainty and take risks. Land's belief in the power of human ingenuity to overcome obstacles was contagious, inspiring those around him to go beyond their perceived boundaries.

Risk-taking was not just a part of Land's philosophy; it was the foundation of his success. He recognized that true innovation frequently necessitated venturing into uncharted territory, where failure was not only possible but probable. However, Land saw failure not as a setback, but as a necessary step on the path to discovery. He famously said, "An essential aspect of creativity is not being afraid to fail." Land believed that every experiment, successful or not, provided valuable insights that informed the next iteration. This mindset enabled him and his teams to overcome numerous challenges, ranging from perfecting the chemistry of instant film to designing cameras that could produce flawless results in real-world conditions.

Land's speeches and writings demonstrate how deeply he believes in the transformative power of creativity. He frequently emphasized the importance of viewing the world not as it is, but as it could be. This forward-looking perspective was central to his innovation process. Land encouraged his teams to envision the ultimate goal—the "impossible" solution—and then work backward to determine the steps required to achieve it. He compared this approach to building a ladder, with each rung representing a small but significant step toward a historic achievement.

Another important aspect of Land's philosophy was his emphasis on multidisciplinary collaboration. He recognized that creativity thrives when people with different perspectives and skills collaborate to solve problems. At Polaroid, Land created an environment in which scientists, engineers, artists, and designers could freely share ideas and challenge one another to think differently. This culture of cross-pollination was critical to the company's success, allowing breakthroughs that would have been impossible in a more siloed environment.

Land also emphasized the role of intuition in the creative process. While he was a scientist who relied on data and experimentation, he frequently emphasized the importance of following one's instincts. He believed that intuition could lead innovators to solutions that are not yet fully understood or articulated. For Land, the interplay of intuition and analysis was a delicate balance that demanded both confidence and humility.

His writings frequently focused on the broader implications of creativity, both for individuals and society as a whole. Land believed that encouraging creativity was essential for progress in all fields, including science, technology, art, and education. He argued for educational systems that valued exploration and discovery, emphasizing the importance of encouraging students to ask questions and think critically. He argued that creativity was a skill that could be developed in anyone.

One of Land's most compelling insights was his conviction in the power of visualization. He frequently described creativity as a process of "seeing the problem and the solution at the same time." His ability to visualize both the challenge and its resolution enabled him to approach problems with clarity and focus. Land's visual thinking extended to his presentations, where he used diagrams, demonstrations, and storytelling to communicate complex ideas in a way that his audience understood.

Land's philosophy of creativity spread beyond Polaroid and into the scientific community. He was a strong supporter of science's role in addressing global issues such as healthcare and environmental sustainability. He believed that creativity was humanity's most valuable asset, capable of transforming not only industries but also the way people lived and interacted with one another.

His approach to problem-solving and innovation left a lasting impression on those who worked with him. Many of his colleagues referred to him as a mentor who encouraged them to think bigger and aim higher. His ability to articulate a vision and rally others around it demonstrated his leadership and in-depth understanding of human nature.

Land's legacy as a creative mind continues to inspire innovators from various disciplines. His ability to combine scientific rigor and creative thinking distinguished him as one of the most influential inventors of his time. He demonstrated to the world that creativity is more than just creating something new; it is also about reimagining possibilities.

In the following chapter, "Facing the Competition," we'll look at the challenges Polaroid faced as the world of photography evolved. From fierce competition with rivals like Kodak to the rise of digital imaging, this chapter will look at how Land and his company navigated an increasingly competitive landscape while remaining committed to their vision of innovation and excellence.

Chapter 11
Facing Competition

For Edwin Land and Polaroid, success in innovation posed unavoidable challenges, the most formidable of which was fierce competition. By the 1970s, Polaroid's instant photography had become a cultural phenomenon, captivating the attention of consumers, artists, and professionals alike. However, the company's success drew competitors eager to capitalize on the thriving market. Among them was Eastman Kodak, a corporate behemoth with deep pockets, decades of experience, and a desire to dominate the photography industry. The battle between Polaroid and Kodak would define this era, putting Land's ingenuity, resilience, and company foundation to the test.

Kodak's entry into the instant photography market represented a direct threat to Polaroid's dominance. For years, Kodak had been a Polaroid partner, providing components such as negatives for its cameras. However, as instant photography gained popularity, Kodak decided to create its own instant camera system. The move signaled the start of a heated rivalry that would result in one of the most famous patent battles in American history.

Polaroid's response to Kodak's challenge was quick and unwavering. Land believed strongly in the value of intellectual property, seeing patents as both a protection for inventors and a recognition of the effort that went into innovation. Polaroid held hundreds of patents for its instant photography technology, which covered everything from the chemical processes of the film to camera mechanics. When Kodak introduced its competing instant camera in 1976, Polaroid filed a lawsuit, claiming that Kodak had infringed 12 of its patents.

The legal battle lasted more than a decade. Both companies poured massive resources into the fight, assembling teams of lawyers, engineers, and scientists to argue their points. For Polaroid, the stakes were huge. Instant photography was more than a product line; it was central to the company's identity and success. Losing the battle with Kodak would have meant losing the market that Polaroid had worked so hard to establish.

Land himself was heavily involved in the litigation, demonstrating his personal commitment to preserving Polaroid's legacy. He saw Kodak's actions as more than just a business challenge; they were a moral affront, an attempt to undermine the principles of innovation and originality that he valued. For Land, the lawsuit was about more than profits; it was about standing up for creators' rights and ensuring that the benefits of innovation went to those who deserved them.

The trial revealed the inner workings of both companies, with lawyers and experts dissecting the intricate details of instant photography technology. Polaroid used the case to demonstrate the ingenuity and complexity of its inventions, reinforcing the company's reputation as a pioneer in the field. Meanwhile, Kodak maintained that its technology was unique and that it had developed its system independently.

After years of court battles, Polaroid was declared the winner in 1986. A federal judge ruled that Kodak had infringed on Polaroid's patents and ordered the company to cease production of instant cameras and film. The decision was significant for both Polaroid and the larger field of intellectual property law. It reaffirmed the importance of protecting innovation and sent a strong message to potential imitators.

Despite the legal victory, Polaroid suffered losses as a result of its battle with Kodak. The lawsuit required significant financial and managerial resources, diverting attention away from other opportunities and challenges. The protracted fight also occurred during a period of rapid change in the photography industry, as digital imaging technologies emerged. While Polaroid was preoccupied with defending its position in instant photography, the seeds of a new revolution were being sown, which would eventually transform the entire industry.

For Land, the Kodak saga was both a triumph and a sobering reminder of the difficulties of leading in a competitive environment. He had founded Polaroid on the principles of innovation, but the fight to protect that innovation required as much determination and strategy as the act of creation. The experience reinforced Land's belief in the value of staying ahead of the curve and constantly pushing the limits of what was possible.

Land was personally affected by his rivalry with Kodak. He was known for his optimism and visionary outlook, but the protracted legal battle drained him. While he remained steadfast in his dedication to Polaroid and its mission, the Kodak case marked a watershed moment in his career. By the end of the trial, Land had begun to step down from his leadership role at Polaroid, leaving the company to navigate an increasingly complex and competitive environment without his direct supervision.

The Kodak battle taught Polaroid and the business world as a whole valuable lesson. It emphasized the significance of intellectual property as a cornerstone of innovation, while also emphasizing the difficulties of maintaining a competitive advantage in a rapidly changing market. The victory reaffirmed Polaroid's status as a photography industry leader, but it also served as a reminder of the importance of adapting and evolving.

In the following chapter, "Trials of Technology," we will look at the challenges that Polaroid faced as digital imaging and other technological shifts became more prevalent. From the company's efforts to innovate in the face of disruption to the legacy of Land's leadership, this chapter will look at how Polaroid navigated the uncertain waters of a shifting industry.

Chapter 12
Trials of Technology

By the late twentieth century, the world of photography was experiencing a seismic shift. Digital technology, once a novel concept, was beginning to transform the industry, promising new ways to capture, store, and share images. For decades, Polaroid was synonymous with innovation and instant photography, a company that revolutionized how people remembered their experiences. However, as digital photography emerged, it presented challenges that tested Polaroid's adaptability and Edwin Land's vision. This period marked the start of Polaroid's demise, a story shaped by the interplay of innovation, resistance, and the relentless march of technological advancement.

Advances in microprocessors, imaging sensors, and memory storage fueled the growth of digital photography in the 1980s and 1990s. Unlike traditional film cameras, digital cameras allow users to take pictures electronically, eliminating the need for physical film and processing. This shift promised unprecedented convenience by allowing photographers to preview and edit their images in real-time. The implications for the photography industry were enormous, as digital technology began to question long-held norms and disrupt established markets.

Polaroid, despite its reputation for being at the cutting edge of innovation, struggled to accept this new reality. Edwin Land, who had built his career by pushing the limits of what was possible, found himself at odds with the industry's trajectory. His attachment to instant film, a medium he had pioneered and perfected, made it difficult for him to fully embrace digital technology. While Polaroid experimented with digital technology, including the development of early digital cameras and printers, these efforts were frequently half-hearted or poorly timed, lacking the bold vision that had defined the company's previous successes.

Land's resistance to digital photography stemmed from his strong attachment to the tactile and immediate qualities of instant film. He believed that the physicality of a Polaroid photograph—holding it, sharing it, and watching it develop in front of one's eyes—was essential to the photographic experience. Land believed that the intangible nature of digital images lacked the emotional resonance of printed photographs, and he was skeptical of a future in which screens would replace paper. While this perspective reflected his passion and dedication to his craft, it also blinded him to digital technology's ability to redefine photography in ways that appealed to a new generation of consumers.

Polaroid's problems were exacerbated by increased competition and the rapid pace of technological change. As Sony, Canon, and Nikon dominated the digital camera market, Polaroid struggled to keep up. Its once-dominant position in the photography industry began to erode as consumers shifted to digital cameras that provided more flexibility and convenience. At the same time, advances in mobile technology and the internet accelerated the transition to digital photography, presenting new opportunities and challenges that Polaroid was unprepared to face.

The company's decline was not solely due to its opposition to digital trends. Polaroid also struggled internally, with mismanagement, financial pressures, and a lack of a cohesive strategy. After Land left Polaroid in 1982, the company struggled to retain its innovative spirit and sense of direction. Without Land's visionary leadership, Polaroid became more reactive, focusing on incremental improvements to existing products rather than pursuing the bold, transformative ideas that defined the company's early years.

The cultural landscape was also shifting, further marginalizing Polaroid. The immediacy of instant photography, once a revolutionary concept, was being surpassed by the instant gratification provided by digital cameras and, later, smartphones. Consumers no longer needed to print their photos; instead, they could view, edit, and share them instantly on screens. Polaroid's core value proposition—instant access to tangible photographs—began to lose relevance as digital sharing became the norm.

By the late 1990s, Polaroid was struggling to remain afloat. The company's efforts to pivot toward digital technology were too late and lacked the coherence required to compete effectively. While Polaroid did introduce digital cameras and other products, it did not capture the market's attention in the same way that its instant cameras had. The company's reliance on legacy products, combined with its failure to fully embrace digital innovation, made it vulnerable to the forces of change.

Land, who had long since left Polaroid, observed the company's decline from the sidelines. For someone who had dedicated his life to innovation and excellence, it was a painful and bittersweet realization. While Polaroid's struggles were partly a reflection of broader industry trends, they also highlighted the difficulties of maintaining innovation in a rapidly changing environment. Land's reluctance to fully embrace digital photography reflected a larger tension between tradition and progress, one that persists in industries dealing with technological disruption.

The demise of Polaroid serves as a cautionary tale about the value of adaptability and foresight in the face of change. While Land's accomplishments and vision catapulted Polaroid to new heights, the company's failure to anticipate and respond to the digital revolution ultimately led to its demise. It was a reminder that even the most innovative companies must constantly reinvent themselves in order to remain relevant, a lesson that has since been repeated across countless industries.

Despite its challenges, Polaroid's legacy endures. The company's innovations in instant photography paved the way for new forms of creativity and self-expression, and their legacy can still be seen in the nostalgia and fascination that surrounds instant cameras today. Edwin Land's vision, while not perfect, continues to inspire innovators and entrepreneurs, providing a powerful example of what is possible when science, art, and imagination come together.

In the following chapter, "A Lifetime of Influence," we will look at Land's lasting legacy, examining how his ideas and innovations influenced not only the photography industry but also the larger worlds of technology, art, and science. This chapter will honor a true visionary's profound and long-lasting contributions, from his influence on future generations of inventors to the cultural significance of his work.

Chapter 13
A Lifetime of Influence

Edwin Land's genius extended far beyond the walls of Polaroid's laboratories and boardrooms, leaving an indelible imprint on photography, art, and technology. His inventions were more than just products; they were cultural milestones that altered how people recorded, shared, and experienced their lives. Throughout his career, Land reimagined the relationship between science and creativity, demonstrating how innovation could inspire and elevate human expression. His influence lives on today, both in the tools we use and in how we think about innovation itself.

The Polaroid instant camera evolved into a cultural icon, not just a technological marvel. The Polaroid Model 95, introduced in 1948, revolutionized photography by making it more immediate, personal, and accessible. For the first time, people could see their photographs in minutes, eliminating the need for film development or dark rooms. This immediacy resonated strongly with users, resulting in a novel photographic experience. Families used Polaroid cameras to capture special moments, artists embraced the technology for its creative potential, and professionals found it invaluable for its practical applications.

The instant camera's influence grew into the world of art, where it became a tool for exploration and experimentation. Ansel Adams, the renowned landscape photographer whose work captures the majesty of the American wilderness, was one of the artists who embraced Polaroid. Adams became a close collaborator and friend of Land, working as a consultant for Polaroid and refining the company's film and camera systems. He praised the instant camera's ability to produce high-quality images with rich detail and tonal range, which were consistent with his meticulous approach to photography. For Adams, Polaroid technology was more than just a convenience; it was a medium that helped him broaden his creative vision.

Andy Warhol, a legendary figure in the pop art movement, was also inspired by Polaroid. Warhol frequently used Polaroid cameras, incorporating instant photographs into his creative process and finished works. The Polaroid format's immediacy and spontaneity suited Warhol's aesthetic, allowing him to capture fleeting moments and turn them into timeless art. Warhol's use of Polaroid technology emphasized its cultural significance, bridging the divide between commercial innovation and high art.

Land's collaborations with artists such as Adams and Warhol demonstrated his belief in the interconnectedness of science and art. He saw photography as both a technical accomplishment and a form of self-expression, and Polaroid as a platform for exploring the intersection of these two worlds. Land frequently discussed the importance of making science more accessible and engaging, and his collaborations with artists demonstrated how technology can inspire new ways of seeing and creating.

The impact of Polaroid technology went beyond the art world, influencing broader cultural trends and norms. The instant camera became a symbol of spontaneity and intimacy, allowing people to capture and share unfiltered moments right away. This quality struck a deep chord in an era before digital photography and social media, providing an unparalleled sense of connection and immediacy.

Polaroid photographs evolved into artifacts of memory, physical objects that could be held, passed around, and displayed. They were used to document everything from family vacations to significant historical events, resulting in a personal and collective visual record of the twentieth century. The distinctive white-bordered prints became instantly recognizable, establishing the brand's identity and demonstrating its enduring appeal.

Land's contributions to photography and art were matched by his influence on technology. Many of the principles and techniques developed at Polaroid, including chemical processing, optics, and materials science, paved the way for progress in other fields. Polaroid's work with instant film, for example, influenced the development of thermal printing and other imaging technologies. Land's ability to translate complex scientific concepts into practical applications influenced a generation of inventors and engineers, shaping the course of innovation in ways that went far beyond photography.

Perhaps Land's greatest legacy is his approach to innovation itself. He believed in the power of curiosity and imagination to drive progress, and he encouraged those around him to take on problems that were "manifestly important and nearly impossible." This philosophy inspired not only his Polaroid teams but also countless others who came across his work and ideas. Land's emphasis on interdisciplinary collaboration, willingness to take risks, and dedication to combining science and art established a benchmark for what innovation could accomplish.

Polaroid's influence lives on in the modern era, where instant photography continues to captivate new generations. The renewed interest in analog formats, fueled by nostalgia and a desire for tangible experiences, has reintroduced Polaroid cameras into the spotlight. The brand's revival reflects Land's vision's timeless appeal, as well as the enduring magic of holding a photograph that develops before your eyes.

When we consider Edwin Land's lifetime of influence, it is clear that his impact was not limited to the products he developed. He transformed people's perspectives on technology and its role in shaping culture, bridging the gap between science and humanity. His work continues to inspire, reminding us that innovation is more than just problem-solving; it is also about expanding possibilities.

In the next chapter, "Beyond Polaroid," we'll look at Land's legacy after he left the company he founded. From his ongoing contributions to science and education to the ways in which his ideas influenced future generations, this chapter will look at how Land's vision extended far beyond the confines of Polaroid, leaving a lasting imprint on the world.

Chapter 14
Beyond Polaroids

Edwin Land's departure from Polaroid in 1982 marked the end of an era for both the individual and the company he founded. After more than four decades of propelling Polaroid to unprecedented heights, Land retired from the corporate world he had transformed. Many found it difficult to imagine Polaroid without its charismatic founder at the helm. For Land, however, this transition represented a new beginning, an opportunity to refocus on the deeper passions that had always driven his work: research, discovery, and the pursuit of knowledge for its own sake.

In the years since his departure, Land has dedicated himself to the Rowland Institute for Science, an independent nonprofit research organization he founded in 1960. Land, freed from the demands of running a global corporation, returned to his favorite work: exploring uncharted scientific territory. The Rowland

Institute reflected Land's belief in the power of curiosity-driven research, providing an environment in which scientists could pursue their most ambitious ideas without being constrained by commercial or academic bureaucracies.

The institute exemplified Land's values of interdisciplinary collaboration and intellectual freedom. Researchers from various fields, including physics, chemistry, and biology, collaborated to solve complex problems and explore new frontiers. Land's innovation philosophy, which is based on creativity, risk-taking, and a commitment to addressing "manifestly important and nearly impossible" challenges, permeated the institute's culture. It was a place where ideas could thrive, unencumbered by immediate concerns about profitability or feasibility.

Although Land no longer led Polaroid, his impact on science and technology remained significant. He continued to push the boundaries of what was possible, delving into topics that piqued his interest, such as advanced optics and molecular biology. Land's work at the Rowland Institute exemplified his unwavering belief in science's ability to illuminate the unknown and improve human life.

Education also became a major focus in Land's later years. He was deeply concerned about the state of science education in the United States, believing that instilling curiosity and critical thinking in young people was critical to the future of innovation. Land frequently emphasized the importance of teaching students not only facts but also the process of discovery itself—the art of asking questions, experimenting, and learning from mistakes. He advocated for an educational system that fostered creativity and encouraged students to view science as a dynamic and exciting pursuit.

Land's dedication to education was evident in his interactions with aspiring scientists at the Rowland Institute and elsewhere. He took a hands-on approach, mentoring researchers and inspiring them to think boldly and ambitiously. For Land, the greatest reward was not the products or accolades his work had earned him, but the opportunity to inspire others to follow their own paths of discovery.

Despite his withdrawal from public life, Land's principles and ideas resonated far beyond the Rowland Institute's walls. The values he promoted—curiosity, creativity, and the fearless pursuit of innovation—remain central to Polaroid's culture and have influenced countless other organizations and individuals. Land's emphasis on interdisciplinary collaboration, in particular, set a precedent for research institutions and businesses looking to foster innovation in an increasingly complex and interconnected world.

Land's legacy was also visible in the continued influence of Polaroid technology and philosophy. The instant camera, once considered a revolutionary invention, had evolved into a cultural icon, inspiring new generations of creators and entrepreneurs. Even as Polaroid struggled to adapt to the digital age, the spirit of innovation that Land instilled in the company survived. His belief that technology should enhance human creativity and connection influenced how people approached the intersection of science and art.

In his later years, Land avoided the spotlight. He preferred to let his work and the work of those he influenced speak for themselves. However, his contributions to science, technology, and education were not unnoticed. Land received numerous honors for his accomplishments, including the Presidential Medal of Freedom in 1963 and membership in the National Academy of Science. These honors demonstrated the profound impact of his work on both his contemporaries and future generations.

Land's approach to innovation—his unwavering curiosity, willingness to take risks, and dedication to combining science and art—continues to inspire those who want to push the boundaries of what is possible. His life's work demonstrates that true innovation entails not only developing new technologies but also reimagining how we see and interact with the world.

As Land's health deteriorated in the late 1980s, he spent more time reflecting on his experiences. For someone who had always been focused on the future, this period provided an opportunity to reflect on the impact he had had. Land's thoughts frequently returned to the people he had collaborated with, the ideas they had pursued together, and the moments of discovery that had defined his career. For Land, the greatest accomplishment was not a single invention, but rather the legacy of creativity and possibility that he had instilled in others.

Edwin Land died in 1991 at the age of 81, leaving behind a body of work that continues to influence the worlds of science, art, and technology. His impact is felt not only through the products and ideas he created but also by the countless people he inspired to think differently and dream bigger.

In the following chapter, "Legacy of a Visionary," we will look at how Land's life and work have continued to resonate in the decades since his death. From Polaroid's enduring cultural significance to the broader lessons of his approach to innovation, this chapter will honor the legacy of a man whose vision and creativity altered the way we see the world.

Chapter 15
The Legacy of A Visionary

Edwin Land's remarkable career and groundbreaking contributions continue to have an impact on the technological and cultural landscapes of the twenty-first century. More than three decades after his death, Land's influence can still be seen in the tools we use, the innovations we celebrate, and how we approach creativity and problem-solving. From the enduring appeal of Polaroid cameras to the ethos of risk-taking and exploration that he promoted, Land's legacy is as vibrant and relevant today as it was during his lifetime.

One of Land's most significant contributions to the world of technology was his pioneering work, which laid the groundwork for many of the advances we now take for granted. The concept of instant gratification, which Polaroid pioneered with its instant cameras, has become a defining feature of the digital era. Today, millions of people use smartphones and social media platforms to capture and share images in real-time, thanks in large part to Land's vision of immediacy and accessibility. Although Polaroid was not a digital company, its spirit of innovation and emphasis on user experience resonate strongly in today's technology industry.

Apple's design approach embodies Land's focus on the smooth integration of hardware, software, and user experience. Steve Jobs, a longtime admirer of Land, frequently cited him as a source of inspiration. Jobs was especially influenced by Land's ability to combine technology and artistry, resulting in products that were as beautiful as they were functional. The similarities between the Polaroid camera and Apple's iconic devices, such as the iPhone, are obvious: both value simplicity, elegance, and an intuitive user interface. In many ways, Land's approach to innovation foreshadowed the current era of personal technology.

Beyond technology, Land's contributions to creativity and the arts have left a lasting impression. The Polaroid instant camera, with its ability to create tangible images in seconds, became a popular tool among artists and photographers all over the world. From Ansel Adams' magnificent landscapes to Andy Warhol's vibrant portraits, Polaroid cameras have been used to create works that capture the immediacy and intimacy of the human experience. The distinct aesthetic of Polaroid photographs—characterized by their unique color palette and instant physicality—inspired countless artists both during Land's lifetime and in the decades that followed.

Even in an era dominated by digital imaging, Polaroid cameras have a nostalgic appeal that reflects their cultural significance. The renewed interest in analog photography, particularly among younger generations, emphasizes the timeless appeal of Land's works. For many people, Polaroid photographs are more than just images; they are artifacts of memory, moments frozen in time that can be held and treasured. This tactile quality, so central to

Land's vision, still resonates in a world where we interact with images primarily through screens.

Historians and technologists alike regard Land as a trailblazer who pushed the limits of what innovation could accomplish. His ability to see the potential in untested ideas and turn them into reality continues to inspire aspiring inventors and entrepreneurs. Land's insistence on addressing "manifestly important and nearly impossible" problems has served as a rallying cry for those who believe in the transformative power of creativity. His work serves as a reminder that progress frequently necessitates boldness, perseverance, and the willingness to accept failure as part of the process.

Land's interdisciplinary approach to innovation, which brought together scientists, engineers, and artists, is another aspect of his legacy that inspires today. At a time when cross-disciplinary collaboration was rare, Land recognized that the best solutions frequently emerged from diverse perspectives. This philosophy has since become a foundation for modern innovation, influencing everything from academic research to corporate strategy.

Technologists who study Land's contributions frequently point out his emphasis on the user experience. For Land, technology was never an end in itself; it was a tool for enhancing human creativity and connection. This user-centric approach, evident in every Polaroid product, is still a guiding principle for many of today's most successful businesses. By prioritizing the user's needs and desires, Land ensured that his inventions were both functional and meaningful.

Artists and creatives continue to honor Land for his contributions to democratizing photography and empowering people to tell their own stories. Prior to the introduction of the Polaroid camera, photography was frequently regarded as a technical and time-consuming process available only to those with specialized skills or resources. Land's instant cameras changed that, making photography more convenient, accessible, and enjoyable. This democratization of the medium not only broadened its reach but also encouraged spontaneity and experimentation, which enhanced the art form.

When discussing Land's life and work, many historians emphasize his visionary nature. Land was not content to simply follow the trends of the time; he sought to redefine them. His ability to anticipate future needs and desires, often before others realized them, distinguished him as a true innovator. Whether through his contributions to optics, photography, or national defense, Land consistently demonstrated the ability to see beyond the horizon, imagining possibilities that others deemed impossible.

However, Land's legacy is not without complexities. His reluctance to fully embrace the digital revolution in the later years of his career exemplifies the difficulties of adjusting to a rapidly changing environment. While Land's devotion to instant film reflected his deep appreciation for its distinct qualities, it also hampered Polaroid's ability to compete in an era defined by digital imaging. This tension between tradition and progress serves as a reminder of the challenges that come with long-term innovation.

Despite these challenges, Land's legacy lives on through the values he championed and the paths he forged. His work demonstrates the power of imagination and the importance of taking calculated risks in order to effect meaningful change. For those who want to make a difference, Land's story provides inspiration and guidance, demonstrating that the greatest accomplishments frequently necessitate venturing into the unknown.

As we look to the future, Land's ideas continue to resonate in ways he could never have predicted. From the renewed interest in analog photography to the ongoing pursuit of seamless user experiences in technology, his legacy lives on in the tools we use, the art we create, and the innovations we strive for. Land's life was a celebration of curiosity, creativity, and the human spirit, leaving a legacy that will undoubtedly inspire future generations.

Conclusion

Edwin Land's life was a shining example of the power of vision and the limitless potential of human ingenuity. From his early fascination with light and optics to the revolutionary inventions that changed the way the world captured its moments, Land's story is one of insatiable curiosity, daring risk-taking, and an unwavering dedication to making the extraordinary possible. His contributions extended far beyond the technical; they addressed the very essence of creativity and the joy of discovery, leaving a legacy that continues to inspire and guide innovators across generations.

Land's quest for "instantaneous innovation" was more than just speed or efficiency; it was about bringing the magic of technology into people's hands and lives in a way that felt natural and transformational. His invention of the Polaroid instant camera was significant not only in photography but also in the history of user-centered design. Land believed that a product's ultimate success depended on its ability to delight and empower the user.

This philosophy of designing with empathy and foresight laid the groundwork for modern technological approaches, influencing countless advances in imaging, optics, and other fields.

The immediacy of the Polaroid camera predicted a world in which instant gratification would become a defining cultural force. Today, we live in an era where images can be captured and shared with the tap of a screen, a reality that Land's innovations helped shape. The principles he promoted—seamless functionality, emotional resonance, and creative freedom—can be found in everything from smartphone cameras to social media platforms. Land may not have lived to witness the entire digital revolution, but his ideas laid the groundwork for the tools and technologies that have transformed how we connect and communicate.

Land's legacy also lives on in optics and imaging, where his breakthroughs in polarizing materials and photographic processes continue to have an impact on advances in healthcare, aerospace, and consumer technology. His insistence on tackling "manifestly important and nearly impossible" challenges has served as a guiding principle for both researchers and entrepreneurs. Land demonstrated to the world that true innovation frequently requires the courage to dream beyond conventional limits, and to imagine solutions that others may dismiss as impossible.

But Land's most profound contribution may be the example he set as a thinker and creator. He believed in the transformative power of curiosity, the importance of asking questions, and the value of failure as a learning opportunity. His life is a reminder that the greatest discoveries are often the result of embracing uncertainty and venturing into the unknown. Land believed that the process of innovation was just as important as the destination—a philosophy that remains relevant in an era of rapid change and technological disruption.

Land's story is more than just a personal triumph; it is a celebration of collaboration and shared vision. At Polaroid, he surrounded himself with brilliant minds from various fields, creating an environment in which ideas could thrive and cross-pollinate. This spirit of interdisciplinary teamwork is still a cornerstone of innovation today, demonstrating the power of bringing together people with diverse perspectives to solve complex problems.

As we consider Land's life and work, it becomes clear that his impact goes far beyond the products he created. He reimagined what it means to be an inventor, combining scientific rigor with artistic sensibility and a profound empathy for the human condition. He demonstrated that technology is about more than just solving problems; it is about enriching people's lives and broadening the horizons of possibility.

In many ways, Land's legacy serves as a call to action. It asks us to think boldly, approach problems with curiosity and imagination, and believe in our ability to make a difference. Whether we are scientists, artists, entrepreneurs, or dreamers, Land's life reminds us that the pursuit of innovation is a collaborative effort that has the potential to change the world.

As we come to the end of this story, it is important to remember the light that Edwin Land carried—not just the literal light of photography and optics, but also the metaphorical light of inspiration and possibility. His journey, marked by vision, perseverance, and a strong desire to discover, serves as a beacon for all who dare to imagine a brighter, more creative future.

Finally, Edwin Land's legacy extends beyond the cameras he invented and the patents he obtained. It is about the ideas he championed, the people he influenced, and the long-term impact of his work on how we see and shape the world. His pursuit of instantaneous innovation was never just about capturing moments; it was about illuminating the path ahead, one bold idea at a time.

May his story inspire us to shine our own light, explore, create, and believe in the extraordinary potential that we all possess. Let us embrace the unknown with courage and curiosity as Edwin Land did, because the future awaits us in the uncharted spaces of possibility.

www.ingramcontent.com/pod-product-compliance
Lightning Source LLC
Chambersburg PA
CBHW071035240526
45469CB00006BD/2221